# An Amazing Star
## The Story of the Wise Men

We are grateful to the following team of authors for their contributions to *God Loves Me,* a Bible story program for young children. This Bible story, one of a series of fifty-two, was written by Patricia L. Nederveld, managing editor for CRC Publications. Suggestions for using this book were developed by Jesslyn DeBoer, a freelance author from Grand Rapids, Michigan. Yvonne Van Ee, an early childhood educator, served as project consultant and wrote *God Loves Me,* the program guide that accompanies this series of Bible storybooks.

Nederveld has served as a consultant to Title I early childhood programs in Colorado. She has extensive experience as a writer, teacher, and consultant for federally funded preschool, kindergarten, and early childhood programs in Colorado, Texas, Michigan, Florida, Missouri, and Washington, using the *High/Scope* Education Research Foundation curriculum. In addition to writing the *Bible Footprints* church curriculum for four- and five-year-olds, Nederveld edited the revised *Threes* curriculum and the first edition of preschool through second grade materials for the *LiFE* curriculum, all published by CRC Publications.

DeBoer has served as a church preschool leader and as coauthor of the preschool-kindergarten materials for the *LiFE* curriculum published by CRC Publications. She has also written K-6 science and health curriculum for Christian Schools International, Grand Rapids, Michigan, and inspirational gift books for Zondervan Publishing House.

Van Ee is a professor and early childhood program advisor in the Education Department at Calvin College, Grand Rapids, Michigan. She has served as curriculum author and consultant for Christian Schools International and wrote the original *Story Hour* organization manual and curriculum materials for fours and fives.

Photo on page 5: SuperStock; photo on page 20: Comstock.

**Library of Congress Cataloging-in-Publication Data**

Nederveld, Patricia L., 1944-
    An amazing star: the story of the wise men/Patricia L. Nederveld.
        p.  cm. — (God loves me; bk. 26)
    Summary:  A simple retelling of the Bible story about the journey
of three wise men to find the baby Jesus. Includes follow-up activities.
    ISBN 1-56212-295-9
    1. Magi—Juvenile literature. [1. Magi.  2. Jesus Christ—Nativity.
    3. Bible stories—N.T.]  I. Title.  II. Series:  Nederveld, Patricia L., 1944-
    God loves me; bk. 26.
    BT315.2.N42   1998
    232.92'3—dc21                                    97-53308
                                                          CIP
                                                           AC

10 9 8 7 6 5 4 3 2 1

# An Amazing Star

## The Story of the Wise Men

PATRICIA L. NEDERVELD

ILLUSTRATIONS BY CATHY ANN JOHNSON

CRC Publications
Grand Rapids, Michigan

# This is a story from God's book, the Bible.

It's for say name(s) of your child(ren). It's for me too!

*Matthew 2:1-12*

"A new star in the sky! Let's follow it," said the wise men one night. "Maybe God wants to lead us to someone special!"

The wise men were right. God was leading them to Jesus.

t was a very long trip. But the star from God helped the wise men find their way.

At last the wise men came to the palace of the king. "We're looking for someone special. Is this where we can find Jesus?" they asked.

"I am the king," said Herod. *"I'm* special!" But the wise men knew God had someone else for them to find.

A gain the star from God led the way—closer and closer to Jesus. The wise men followed it to Bethlehem. "Can Jesus be here?" they wondered.

**Y**es! The star
from God
brought
them right to the
house where little
Jesus lived with
Mary and Joseph.

When the wise men found Jesus, they gave him wonderful presents. For they knew that God had led them to someone very special—Jesus, God's own Son.

**I** wonder if you'd like to say thank you to God for sending baby Jesus . . .

*Dear God, thank you for sending baby Jesus! We're glad you love us so much. Amen.*

# Suggestions for Follow-up

## Opening

The predictability of regular routines gives children a sense of order and security. By keeping the usual patterns in your time together, you'll be helping your little ones enjoy the Christmas season.

Provide a simple nativity scene for your children to use for retelling the Christmas story. As you gather in a group, ask the children if they remember who was born in a manger and who brought the good news to the shepherds. Prompt them to say the good news: "Jesus, God's own Son, is born!" Repeat the good news three or four times, each time a little louder until the good news becomes a cheer. Wonder with the children who else will find out about the good news.

## Learning Through Play

Learning through play is the best way! The following activity suggestions are meant to help you provide props and experiences that will invite the children to play their way into the Scripture story and its simple truth. Try to provide plenty of time for the children to choose their own activities and to play individually. Use group activities sparingly—little ones learn most comfortably with a minimum of structure.

1.  Invite children to act out parenting roles in your dramatic play center. As they care for baby dolls, remind them that Jesus was a baby—a very special baby, God's own Son. Encourage them to pretend it is someone's birthday, and ask your little ones if they remember whose birthday we celebrate at Christmas time. Set out a few simple decorations, baking tools, gift bags, and wrapping paper and bows to help them pretend they are getting their house ready for Christmas. Explain how the special things we do every year at Christmas remind us of the birth of Jesus.

2.  Help your little ones build fancy tall palaces and simple small houses with building blocks. Wonder with the children where they would most likely find a very important person living. Share your own wonder and amazement that Jesus, God's very own Son, didn't live in a big fancy house. Remind the children about the stable where Jesus was born and the tiny house where Jesus lived with Joseph and Mary.

3.  Provide materials for children to make Christmas ornaments. Copy and cut out the wise man and star figures (Pattern L, Patterns Section, *God Loves Me* program guide). Set out crayons or washable markers, and invite the children to color them. Older children will enjoy adding glitter to the star. Show the children how to rub a glue stick around the edges or all over the star, shake the glitter over the glue, and wiggle the star until the glitter sticks. Punch a hole at the top of each ornament, and string yarn or ribbon through the hole to make a hanger.

4.  Invite your little ones and their families to bring small baby rattles, teething rings, pacifiers, booties, and the like to decorate the

Christmas tree in your room. These can be old favorites the children enjoyed as babies. Label each item with the child's initials, add ribbon hangers, and help the children hang them on the tree. You may prefer to request brand-new items to give to a new baby in your church. Invite the new mother to bring the baby for your little ones to admire, and let them give their gifts to the baby. Remind your little ones that Jesus was a very special baby—God's own Son!

5.  Play the game "Follow the Star." Make a large star from cardboard, and cover it with aluminum foil or gold wrapping paper. Invite children to follow your actions as you sing these words to the tune of "We're Following the Leader" (from *Peter Pan*):

> *We're following the star, the star, the star.*
> *We're following the star, wherever it might go.*
> (March around the room as you hold the star.)
> *We found the baby Jesus, Jesus, Jesus.*
> *We found the baby Jesus. He's special, you know!*
> (Rock folded arms as if holding a baby.)
> *Thank you, God, for Jesus, Jesus, Jesus.*
> *Thank you, God, for Jesus! We're glad you love us so!*
> (Fold hands and bow head.)

## Closing

Teach your little ones the simple song "God Loved Us" (tune: "London Bridge"), and add the actions after you've sung it a time or two.

> *God loved us* (point up and then to self)
> *and sent his son,* (rock folded arms as if holding a baby)
> *sent his son,* (continue rocking arms)
> *sent his son.* (continue rocking arms)
> *God loved us* (point up and then to self)
> *and sent his son—*(rock folded arms as if holding a baby)
> *baby Jesus!* (sing softly with chin resting on folded hands)

—Adapted from "God Loved Us," Preschool Page, November/December 1996. Reprinted by permission from *Children's Ministry Magazine,* © 1996, Group Publishing, Box 481, Loveland, CO 80539.

---

### At Home

During the busy holiday season, take short breaks to sit with your little one. Share your wonder that God gave you and your family a very precious gift—baby Jesus, his own Son. Read a book, listen to music, look at the lights on the tree, and enjoy a quiet time together.

## Old Testament Stories

**Blue and Green and Purple Too!** *The Story of God's Colorful World*

**It's a Noisy Place!** *The Story of the First Creatures*

**Adam and Eve** *The Story of the First Man and Woman*

**Take Good Care of My World!** *The Story of Adam and Eve in the Garden*

**A Very Sad Day** *The Story of Adam and Eve's Disobedience*

**A Rainy, Rainy Day** *The Story of Noah*

**Count the Stars!** *The Story of God's Promise to Abraham and Sarah*

**A Girl Named Rebekah** *The Story of God's Answer to Abraham*

**Two Coats for Joseph** *The Story of Young Joseph*

**Plenty to Eat** *The Story of Joseph and His Brothers*

**Safe in a Basket** *The Story of Baby Moses*

**I'll Do It!** *The Story of Moses and the Burning Bush*

**Safe at Last!** *The Story of Moses and the Red Sea*

**What Is It?** *The Story of Manna in the Desert*

**A Tall Wall** *The Story of Jericho*

**A Baby for Hannah** *The Story of an Answered Prayer*

**Samuel! Samuel!** *The Story of God's Call to Samuel*

**Lions and Bears!** *The Story of David the Shepherd Boy*

**David and the Giant** *The Story of David and Goliath*

**A Little Jar of Oil** *The Story of Elisha and the Widow*

**One, Two, Three, Four, Five, Six, Seven!** *The Story of Elisha and Naaman*

**A Big Fish Story** *The Story of Jonah*

**Lions, Lions!** *The Story of Daniel*

## New Testament Stories

**Jesus Is Born!** *The Story of Christmas*

**Good News!** *The Story of the Shepherds*

**An Amazing Star!** *The Story of the Wise Men*

**Waiting, Waiting, Waiting!** *The Story of Simeon and Anna*

**Who Is This Child?** *The Story of Jesus in the Temple*

**Follow Me!** *The Story of Jesus and His Twelve Helpers*

**The Greatest Gift** *The Story of Jesus and the Woman at the Well*

**A Father's Wish** *The Story of Jesus and a Little Boy*

**Just Believe!** *The Story of Jesus and a Little Girl*

**Get Up and Walk!** *The Story of Jesus and a Man Who Couldn't Walk*

**A Little Lunch** *The Story of Jesus and a Hungry Crowd*

**A Scary Storm** *The Story of Jesus and a Stormy Sea*

**Thank You, Jesus!** *The Story of Jesus and One Thankful Man*

**A Wonderful Sight!** *The Story of Jesus and a Man Who Couldn't See*

**A Better Thing to Do** *The Story of Jesus and Mary and Martha*

**A Lost Lamb** *The Story of the Good Shepherd*

**Come to Me!** *The Story of Jesus and the Children*

**Have a Great Day!** *The Story of Jesus and Zacchaeus*

**I Love You, Jesus!** *The Story of Mary's Gift to Jesus*

**Hosanna!** *The Story of Palm Sunday*

**The Best Day Ever!** *The Story of Easter*

**Goodbye—for Now** *The Story of Jesus' Return to Heaven*

**A Prayer for Peter** *The Story of Peter in Prison*

**Sad Day, Happy Day!** *The Story of Peter and Dorcas*

**A New Friend** *The Story of Paul's Conversion*

**Over the Wall** *The Story of Paul's Escape in a Basket*

**A Song in the Night** *The Story of Paul and Silas in Prison*

**A Ride in the Night** *The Story of Paul's Escape on Horseback*

**The Shipwreck** *The Story of Paul's Rescue at Sea*

## Holiday Stories

Selected stories from the New Testament to help you celebrate the Christian year

**Jesus Is Born!** *The Story of Christmas*

**Good News!** *The Story of the Shepherds*

**An Amazing Star!** *The Story of the Wise Men*

**Hosanna!** *The Story of Palm Sunday*

**The Best Day Ever!** *The Story of Easter*

**Goodbye—for Now** *The Story of Jesus' Return to Heaven*

These fifty-two books are the heart of *God Loves Me,* a Bible story program designed for young children. Individual books (or the entire set) and the accompanying program guide *God Loves Me* are available from CRC Publications (1-800-333-8300).